Introduction

Congratulations! You have taken a positive step fo
copy of this book. I wrote this book because I want
better place by taking notes of people's bad personalities and putting them
all in a book; because as obvious as they are, some people do not know that
their behaviors irritate their surroundings. If a friend suggested you this
book, it does not necessarily mean that you are an annoying person to
him/her; it just means that he or she wants you to become a better person,
in case any of these 44 things apply to you.

Table of contents

Introduction

Table of contents

How to use this book

Social tips you should know

1. Not everybody is your family
2. Friends, not maids
3. From friends to slaves
4. They don't have to like your gifts
5. "Hey look at this"
6. "I'm interesting, you're not"
7. "Trust me, I'm an engineer"
8. Talking about everyone's flaws when you're actually full of it
9. "I like waiting" said no one ever
10. Armpits from hell & the devil's barbecue
11. "How dare you oppose a rich man?"
12. "I hate girls with selfies like this"
13. Mr. Blame

14. Repeating others' jokes
15. Only the dead knows peace from this
16. This house isn't a nightclub
17. "It's good but…"
18. FBI-ing
19. "My interests are better than yours"
20. "Do you and your girlfriend…"
21. Friends first… or was it smartphones first?
22. Whose toenail is this?
23. Your friend loves you, but only for three hours
24. "Did I die?"
25. "I'm fat, so is this hamburger"
26. "Hey look, John's zippers are open!"
27. Stop means Stop in English
28. Not everybody should wake up at 4am
29. Cell phones don't need oil massage
30. Movies are not meant to be interrupted
31. Computer screens don't giggle
32. "Tonight, we're eating cell phones."
33. Showing off your friend's belongings to your friends
34. Mr. CEO's secretary
35. A thumbs up isn't worth a thousand words
36. "You think you had a bad day? Last time I…"
37. "I used to be good at drawing too"
38. Adult manners should be child manners
39. "Our toilet, my rules"

40.	"I'll buy you another one / I'll replace it later"
41.	"They don't use it right away, therefore, they don't care about it"
42.	"It's free because he's my friend"
43.	Just answer their question, it's their decision
44.	"No offence" means "I'm going to hurt you"

Conclusion

How to use this book
The chapters in this book are not in order so you can skip to whichever chapter you currently want to read. Each chapter has a small introduction to let you know what we are going to be talking about, and then there is the body, which is often a short example story. At the end of a chapter, you will find a short overview of the chapter (if you are lazy to read the book, you can just skip to the overview, but I recommend you to read the whole chapter!).

Social tips you should know
Now before we get started with the long list of annoying behaviors to avoid, I would like to give you some valuable base tips that you can use to improve your everyday life without having to always read a long list of annoying habits to figure out if something is considered annoying or not.

Emotional forecasting: The concept of emotional forecasting (as I like to call it) is simple; you analyze your audience (one person or more) and try to predict the emotional outcome of any action you do or words you say to that audience. If you say something to a certain person, will the person be happy or sad? You need to tailor your words in such a way that you never offend anyone; saying things such as "that dress looks too young-looking on you" will offend the person as it sounds like you're calling the person old.

Peeve list / Blacklist: This trick involves taking notes in your head whenever someone does something that you find annoying. This way, you build a "to-not-do" list in your head that you keep in handy for when you are around your friends; you will then know what behaviors to avoid since those behaviors already annoyed you before.

Analyze your day: Sometimes we do some things that we don't consider annoying but are obviously irritating to our surroundings, we might not even know that we're being offensive during a conversation. That is the reason I wrote a long list of what behaviors to avoid and how to fix them; however, even with the following list, when the day ends I want you to think of the conversations you had during the day and try to analyze the actions you did and see what could've been annoying to your friends and how you could improve them.

Those are just the basics of what will get you started. Positive self-consciousness is important when performing any social action so that you always know where things are going. Now let's move on and start reviewing the common irritating behaviors you should avoid or stop doing.

1. Not everybody is your family

Do you constantly complain about your life and problems to your co-workers? Well, there is nothing wrong with talking to your friends about your problems; in fact, it is a great way to get some relief and get something off your chest since holding all of your feelings and problems inside will only result in tension building up inside you, and it might cause you to "explode" at some point, resulting in some negative actions; however, problem sharing can develop into a bad habit as you can get addicted to having your friends and co-workers listen to you and cheer you up.

Keep track of the number of times you have been complaining to your friends and keep it to a minimum.

You and your friends/colleagues are like a fruit, if one part starts to rot, it will eventually spread throughout the whole body. The same goes for you, if you constantly complain about your life to your friends, especially when you say things like "life is unfair", "it would be better if the world ended" etc., you will end up rotting them as well by spreading negativity around the whole place and you will end up turning them into another version of yourself.

I recommend you to choose when to share and who you share your problems with. Only talk about it every now and then, people have their problems too and only a few will understand you clearly.

To recap this chapter,

Don't constantly complain about your life to everyone.

2. Friends, not maids

Do you often leave a pile of mess and then have your friends/family/co-workers clean it up for you? If so, then you should break that habit as soon as you can; the people around you don't tell you, but they find it annoying, and it makes people lose respect for you since it is an immature move.

Let's take the example of an irritating fast food employee, let's name him Jack; Jack is always wild at work, he puts the utensils in unusual places and leaves the tables full of oil, mustard and ketchup. When his hours end, he rushes home with only the money on his mind and the other workers have to clean it all up, the next day comes and he does the same thing over and over again. Jack's co-workers are tired of that annoying behavior; they might even agree to save up for a voodoo doll and cast an evil spell on Jack if he doesn't stop (well, they're not actually going to do that).

Let's take another example, you have a jobless young uncle and he is always in your living room since the game console and TV is there, he brings his Coke can and bag of chips in that room and leaves everything on the table when he's done. It's always you that cleans up his mess, and he won't do it if you just leave it there. When he comes back after taking a walk, he makes a big mess again and if you talk to him about it, he's going to give a flat reply like "what can I do? Putting it away every time is too tiring…" you face palm and secretly wish you could kick him out.

The lesson: You should always clean up after you make a mess (and you should be aware that you've made a mess in the first place). Never leave leftover plates, cans and other things all around the place and always make sure to be organized at work since you wouldn't want your co-workers to always clean up any mess you leave, as if you were some sort of king ready to be served and taken care of all the time.

To recap this chapter,

Don't make a mess out of your room/office/workplace and expect people to always cleanup for you.

3. From friends to slaves

This time, we'll be talking about the habit of asking too much favors and turning people into errand boys/girls.

Do you have somebody that you constantly ask for favors? It can be someone who is younger than you, someone that looks free, some other person's child or someone that can potentially offer something you need. It can happen in our daily lives that we end up asking too much favors because we forget that the person has a life and obligations too.

Susan is a mother, her daughter is married to a man called Tim; Tim is a hardworking businessman who has a nice car and earns enough from his hard work. Whenever Susan needs to go somewhere, she asks Tim to give her a ride, whenever Susan needs money, she asks Tim to lend her some. Tim loves Susan because she is the mother of his wife, but Tim does not appreciate the fact that Susan relies entirely on him for all of her needs.

Another example, let's say that Bob and Mark are co-workers. Bob has a bad habit of spending all of his money a few days after receiving his paycheck so he always asks Mark to lend him some and tells Mark that he will give it back at the end of the month. A onetime favor would be okay if Bob had his reasons to spend the money, but when the next month comes, Bob does the same thing and the cycle goes on. Mark feels frustrated because he had some plans with the money and he feels like he's a slave working for Bob.

A third example would be about a person who constantly asks his/her little sister/cousin to go out and buy him/her some things, even if they're still young and look free, you might have interrupted their precious free time that they chose to spend doing something important to them.

Do not ask for too many favors, you need to understand that people all have a life too no matter how much time and money you think they have. Whatever excuse you are using, don't think that they will always be at your service; manage your needs as much as you can so you don't have to disturb other people to do things for you.

To recap this chapter,

Don't ask for too much favors to the point where your friends are turned into errand boys/girls.

4. They don't have to like your gifts

So maybe you realized that your behaviors were sort of annoying to your surroundings, you want to make up for it and decide to give them a small gift, let's say a cupcake. This is a very good move since this often makes people cool down and think "hey, maybe I was too rude being mad at him, he's not really a bad guy after all, he just sometimes does irritating things... this cupcake is not bad either", but what happens when you start to turn it into a habit? It becomes annoying as well, because sooner or later, they will feel forced to eat your cupcakes and forced to forgive your never-ending habit just because you're feeding them creamy pastry.

The fix: Locate the source of your problem, your bad habits, and leave those habits so you won't even have the need to make up for anything. If your neighbor gave you cookies as an apology for having their dog poop on your front yard, this does not mean that you will be okay with receiving cookies every day, asking you to allow their dog to continue its usual routine.

To recap this chapter,

Don't give gifts/money to make up for your bad behaviors, fix them.

5. "Hey look at this"

This is a common behavior that you see in children, they want your attention whenever something amazes them. It can be something that's not that interesting, but it means so much to them. Let's say your niece is watching cartoons and you are on your computer concentrating on something, whenever something interesting happens on her screen, she's going to bump you with her little hand and point at the screen, giggling and saying "Look! The funny monster is angry!" you smile and say "Aw is that so? Yes he looks very angry". But what happens when she does it too often? It starts to get a little annoying and you cannot concentrate on your own things.

This happens in adults too, they grow up and whatever is interesting to them just changes, but it's the same thing, whenever they find something amazing, they want to show it to their surroundings, they love it so much that they want other people to know how great their interest is.

So let's take an example, you are working in a call center and everyone gets a computer with internet access. You have a lazy co-worker that sits right beside you, he only works one third of the day and spends the rest watching snowboarding videos; whenever some cool trick is being performed in his video, he pats your arm and point to his screen saying "hey check this out, check this out!" you look at his screen and say "whoa, sick!", you then turn back to your screen and reply to some emails until he pulls you again and says "how 'bout this one?!", you watch the trick being performed and murmur a less enthusiastic "whoa", and it goes on until the workday ends. There's no denying that the video was great and that the tricks were sick, but you had your own things to do and you needed to concentrate during that day.

The lesson for this chapter is to never repetitively bother people with things that you find interesting, it is okay to show them every once in a while, but if you do it repetitively, you're going to end up breaking their concentration and get them angry instead of being "happily amazed" at whatever you're showing them.

To recap this chapter,

Don't always ask people to look at something you find interesting.

6. "I'm interesting, you're not"

This phenomenon occurs when you are hanging out with a friend and you two are with a group of people or with a person that you indirectly want to impress. The human instinct for chasing authority kicks in and you do anything to look your best in the eyes of the person you want to impress.

Let's take the example of three young people, we'll name them Chad, Steve and Kate. The three are classmates and they usually walk home together after school, Kate is always in the middle and the boys are on each of her sides. Kate always talks to both of them, but whenever Kate talks to Steve, Chad always tries his best to find flaws in Steve's words and bash him using his own words so that Steve looks bad in front of Kate and only Chad would look like the nice one to hang out with, Chad wants Kate's attention to be all his and Chad goes as far as telling offensive jokes about Steve.

Anything Steve says will be used against him, if Steve says that he plays the violin, Chad is going to jokingly say that violin is for girls and it hurts Steve, it also annoys him because every time they're with Kate, Chad always puts on this annoying attitude.

Whenever you're with a friend and there's someone you want to impress, never put your friend down; instead, work it out on your own, make yourself look impressive without having to use negative tactics on the other person you're "competing" with. This sort of behavior (that I like to call "defensive narcissism") is really irritating to some people and it also gives pressure when it's recurring (for example, every time Chad walks home with Steven and Kate).

To recap this chapter,

Never put someone down just to make yourself look better in front of some people.

7. "Trust me, I'm an engineer"

Let's say you are in a group of people, whenever you and your friends are amazed at something, one friend comes in and explains the currently discussed phenomenon. He does this all the time, he (or she) acts like he knows it all. Sometimes he's right, and sometimes the things he says are not completely true but he keeps talking about it anyways because he wants to sound interesting.

You've had one friend like this, or maybe you are that friend; being a know-it-all can be satisfying at times because you feel mighty and intelligent explaining everything about the topic that you know very well; it gives you self-confidence because it's something you're really good at and it will let people know that you have some knowledge and qualities. You also do this because you love learning and you want to release all the knowledge trapped in your head; of course, the only way to do that for you is to talk about all of it to the people around you.

Why is it annoying? It is annoying because sometimes it makes people feel less superior than you are, sometimes it makes you look narcissistic, and sometimes it makes people secretly whisper "but nobody asked you…" in their heads, especially when you do this every time you're with people.

When you speak, avoid introductions such as "Actually…" and "Well…" as it makes you sound more of a know-it-all than you already do; also, only explain some things when asked.

To recap this chapter,

Don't explain everything in sight without anyone asking just to look smart.

8. Talking about everyone's flaws when you're actually full of it

It happens very often that we point the flaws of other people without even realizing ours; sometimes we do realize that we also have our bad habits and mistakes, but the way we talk about other people sometimes makes it sound as if we were angels ourselves. There are different types of flaws and it can be physical, psychological, social or something else.

Say you talk to your friend about something and she interrupts you midway, you get mad because your point isn't proven yet, so you immediately tell her "Please for once, listen to the person until the end before you talk back. I hate it when people do this.", even if you're right, you should make sure that you're not the one who always does what you just corrected her about.

Another example, say you hang out with two friends, let's name them Mike and Dave; Dave says he's going to go home because it's late, so you two let him go; when Dave is gone, you start talking to Mike about every single flaw Dave has. Mike is probably Dave's secret best friend; he knows that Dave isn't perfect but he feels hurt because you talk like if you were backstabbing Dave.

Are you their mother/father? Remember, despite having an obsession for details, you should not correct everyone like if you were a perfect example yourself. Talking behind people's backs with your friends will create a distance between you and your friends since they might not like your bad habit of backstabbing as well, and it brings negativity to their lives.

Know that some people have flaws that they can't control; for example, a person who constantly coughs might appear rude to you, but they might have some unknown sickness that gave them that problem. A lot of people sooner or later end up realizing their flaws and try to change for the better (maybe they're going to read this book someday) so you don't have to always act like Mr. or Mrs. Behavior police.

If you really feel the need to change them, then point and correct them to the right way without necessarily telling them that they're wrong.

To recap this chapter,

Don't point the flaws of the people you know like if you don't have any.

9. "I like waiting" said no one ever

Have you ever arranged a meet-up with a friend and have that friend come an hour late? Some people think that "meet me at 9 a.m." means anywhere between 9:00 and 9:59 (as long as there's a "9" in the numbers). As obvious as this sounds, getting stuck waiting for someone is really annoying and I made sure to write a chapter about it.

You tell your friend to meet you at 10pm outside the café; she insists that you two should meet at 9pm. When the time really comes, she's not even at the meeting place yet. You spend five minutes, ten minutes, thirty minutes and up to an hour waiting for her. After an hour, you finally see her and she's walking slow and peacefully towards you, still having the time to stop and carefully remove the salad from her morning sandwich before continuing her route. You don't even need to ask but she will give you a silly excuse and do as if nothing wrong happened, since she's here now.

You should work hard on your habits (your morning routine etc.) to minimize your "getting-ready" time and do your best to get to your meet-ups and appointments in time. When you make people wait, you're giving them frustration, making them feel as if one minute is as long as an hour.

To recap this chapter,

Arrive in time when you have an appointment or should meet-up with someone.

10. Armpits from hell & the devil's barbecue

This chapter is pretty straightforward and the title says it all. Take a shower as often as you can and make sure to put some deodorant or anything that will prevent you from smelling in public. Do not smoke in closed areas and crowded places as this can really irritate your surroundings.

I remember when I was younger; I had an internship as a webmaster in an advertising company, I had a co-worker (let's call him Bob so he doesn't recognize himself, just in case he reads this book) the room we were in was very small and we barely had any air to breathe but Bob kept on smoking each and every day, he would smoke until either his pack ran empty or the day ended. I really hated it that time, I could barely breathe and it always gave me a headache; whenever I would tell him, he would just giggle and say "well sorry kid" and keep going.

Don't be like Bob, seriously, if you're going to smoke, analyze the environment first if there's anyone next to you (unless you all smoke in the room, that's a totally different story), the best thing to do is to tell them that you're going to smoke and to ask them if it is okay with them.

We should not really judge a person by their smell, but a lot of people won't feel comfortable around you if your cigarette's smoke is the new oxygen, and your armpits smell like pure apple cider vinegar. You don't have to spray deodorant and perfume every five minutes but just make sure that you're not purposely smelly.

To recap this chapter,

Always make sure you have good hygiene and are pleasing to be around, ask before smoking.

11. "How dare you oppose a rich man?"

Whether you get into an argument, line up for something or do something else, you should never use your authority to justify yourself.

Some time ago, I was with this friend that came from Germany; he was a web developer that earned six figures a year and he was pretty much the kind of guy that was living the dream. One day, we were at a café and he took a smoke while waiting for our order, the waitress kindly asked him to put his cigarette down because it was disturbing the other customers; shortly after that, they kind of got into a small dispute since he was hard headed and we had to leave the café in the end. As we walked outside, he said the words "how dare she oppose me when she's just some poor waitress in this poor country"; at that time, I lost some of my respect for him and started to feel apathy towards working with him.

No matter how wealthy you are or where you come from, your financial and social success does not necessarily make you a better human than anyone you believe to be below you. If you keep saying "how dare she talk to me like that, does she know how high/wealthy I am?", you are going to end up annoying your friends since they are probably not as "high" as you are and they can relate more to the person you were against.

To recap this chapter,

Never say or think that you have more authority because you came from a special place or have more wealth.

12. "I hate girls with selfies like this"
This chapter has similarities with a previous one you've read (pointing people's flaws when you're full of it), except that this one is about generally criticizing other people, and other people's friends.

Imagine that you had a friend (let's name him Dean!); a friend that you are very close to, you two play games together and "make fun of people" together because you two always thought that you were the coolest people on the planet; but lately, you've read a cool book (this book) and learned that criticizing people isn't such a fun thing to do; you don't point out people's flaws anymore whenever you're with Dean, but he still does it, whenever you two get together and you browse your Facebook newsfeed, he sometimes stares at your screen and says things like "Ha-ha, that guy looks weird", "ha-ha, that girl's hair looks like a broccoli", "Pfff.. I hate girls who take selfies like these" and so on, but what Dean doesn't realize is that those people are all friends of yours (it was your newsfeed after all), maybe one of them was even your girlfriend and you feel hurt by Dean's comments. You tell Dean to stop and he gives you a weird face as a reply because you two used to do that together, and he doesn't know why you would ever tell him to stop (he thought it was fun!).

Don't be like Dean; don't criticize people around you or on your friend's screen because those might be your friend's close friends, it puts a barrier between you and your friend because your friend might value those close friends a lot and it hurts to hear your words.

To recap this chapter,

Never criticize people that your friend knows/people on their screen as it might be your friend's close friend or even their girlfriend/boyfriend.

13. Mr. Blame

Do you know someone that never thinks they're wrong but blames every little problem on the people around? Or is that person you? If that's the case, then you should stop.

You know how it usually goes; your boss asks you to write an important email that you're supposed to send to a future associate for partnership, but you're too lazy to do it, so you ask another co-worker (one that has nothing to do with it) to write it for you. Your co-worker knows nothing about it and spends half of the day researching about the specific topic, in the end, he manages to do it but the email wasn't so convincing and the potential partnership with the future associate is lost. Your boss comes in the office and yells at you for writing such an amateur email, you then point at your co-worker with your finger nearly pressed on his face and tell your boss that the guy said he'd help you write it and that he's the one who messed it all up; your friend gets fired and you look for your next victim next time something similar happens.

Let's take another example, your mother asks you to turn the stove off after ten minutes, you then ask your little brother to remind you to turn it off after ten minutes; when the time comes, your brother forgets to remind you about it and the special Taiwanese soup your mother has been preparing is now burned since you forgot to take it off the stove. After your mother comes and yells at you, you blame your brother for not reminding you and now he's locked in his room, crying and temporarily hating you.

Putting the blame on people when it's something you should've taken care of is an immature move and it also puts distance between you and that person since it's hurtful and it also makes you look like you did not have any responsibility in it at all.

To recap this chapter,

Don't always look for people to blame for the unfortunate events you might be responsible for.

14. Repeating others' jokes

This will be a short chapter and it is about those times where one person says a very nice joke but the group of people he is in is making too much noise to even hear it, a friend then decides to repeat the joke in a louder voice, causing everyone to pause and look at him silently before they burst out into laughter and praise him. The person who came up with the original joke then pretends to laugh while feeling all left out and upset about it.

If you thought that your friend's joke was funny and you want everyone to hear it, repeat it in a louder voice and tell them afterwards that your friend was the one who came up with it. This way, everyone gets a smile, you get to tell the joke and your friend is credited.

To recap this chapter,

Don't take credit for other's jokes, repeat it and let people know who said it first.

15. Only the dead knows peace from this

This is the one that I hate the most, it is when you are sleeping nicely (or are still trying to find sleep) and someone is still up late at night playing music or games or whatever thing that vibrates sound waves. I have insomnia and sleep is very valuable for me so these kinds of things irritate me the most because I can never find sleep when this happens and I wake up very tiredly in the morning.

Let's elaborate, you are somebody who doesn't like sleeping late or being disturbed at night, but your homeless uncle (he's back!) is always staying up late and he plays music loudly in his room where you can still hear him, you roll around in bed frustrated since you can't find sleep (the guy is even singing along). That's not just it, one hour after that, the music finally stops, and you think that it is finally over but he then opens the creaky doors in the hall making all kinds of noises as he enters the kitchen to eat some of your bread and mayonnaise; when he comes back, he slams the door loudly like a real champ and goes back to his room. You start questioning his existence and want to explode as you look at the time; you can't do anything but wait until he finally goes to sleep.

Don't be like that uncle, please don't.

If you really need to listen to music, use your headphones. If you're feeling hungry at night, prepare some sealed food and bring it to your room before everyone's bedtime.

To recap this chapter,

Never wake up at night and disturb anyone that's sleeping and don't make any noise even if you're in another room.

16. This house isn't a nightclub

This is also one of the things really irritates me, when you're concentrated on reading a book, writing, or doing something that requires you to pay attention and someone suddenly blasts their favorite song with their laptop/phone, you lose all the attention you had and it creates a negative response in your brain that results in anger and frustration.

When you see that someone shouldn't be disturbed, use headphones; when you see that a group of people is having a peaceful time, do not play music or videos loudly; lastly, when somebody is sleeping, never disturb them, never!

"But I have to watch this important video, what do I do?" Well the answer is simple and was already stated above: use headphones, you really don't want to anger anyone by blasting your music out loud next to someone who wants to have a peaceful time.

To recap this chapter,

Always use headphones, never blast music or videos/movies in a calm or public place.

17. "It's good but..."

This one has similarities, but is different from that one chapter about your friend that always criticizes the people around you. The difference is that this one is about criticizing the things you find interesting, or about you criticizing what others find interesting. Generally, it is about criticizing everything.

You are hanging out with a friend (again!) and you walk past a nice car that you find amazing. You turn to your friend and tell him "hey look at that car, I love it!" he looks at it and says "yeah, it's good but most sports cars are for the rich people who spends money on expensive things", you then silently turn back to the road and continue your walk. After some time, you see a girl that you knew from school and tell your friend that you find her beautiful; after seeing her, he then tells you "well... She's cute but her lips look too big". Lastly, you walk past a fashion store and you tell him that you would like to own a jacket like the one on display, he gives you the answer of "well it's not like I want to criticize but I don't really know what people find good in those jackets... well yeah, I know everyone has their preferences but for me, I don't find them to be that good". You then learn your lesson and never tell him anymore when you find something to be nice.

So for this chapter's lesson, if somebody wants to show you something, it means that they find it great and that it means something to them. Don't criticize it even if you find a lot of flaws in whatever they find interesting, or you will just end up hurting them. As the main keyword of this book says, it is really an annoying behavior.

To recap this chapter,

Don't criticize everything; don't criticize the things that others find interesting.

18. FBI-ing

We've all been through this, either you are the one who snooped on somebody's phone or the one who has had his/her phone snooped on, there's no denying that it is indeed a bad thing produced by curiosity, and it is a violation of someone's privacy.

You're on the couch. Your friend went to shower. His phone is sitting on the pillow right beside you. You already know that he would never find out if you were checking out his messages. You think about it for five minutes and decide to do it. Thirty minutes have passed and you put the phone down. You start thinking that it was maybe a bad idea, and now, your face is full of guilt and regret.

It is natural that we feel curious at some time, especially if the person is your partner or spouse; you however need to know that snooping on their phone is wrong and that you should talk to them if there is something that bothers you about them (You're afraid that they are being unfaithful for example).

By snooping on someone else's messages and files, you may also end up discovering things that you should not be seeing, be it passwords, friends' private pictures or confidential business information.

You wouldn't want someone to search through your phone, messages and computer while you're away would you? Remember that it's wrong, and learn to control yourself whenever someone leaves their devices vulnerable to you.

To recap this chapter,

Never, ever spy pictures and messages in your friend's phone or computer when he or she is away.

19. "My interests are better than yours"

This chapter shares common features with a previous chapter ("It's good but..."). This time, it is about those times where one person criticizes another person's interests because they like different things.

Let's say that you live in a period where two music genres are being the mainstream thing. One is Spanish music, and the other one is Italian music. You're in love with Spanish music, the singers are a bit conservative and the songs are calm and soft. Your friend on the other hand (Let's name her Victoria) loves Italian music and she likes the way Italian guys perform, they are muscled, their songs are faster paced and there's dancing in all of their music videos; they are also topless 90% of the time (well it might not be the case in real life but this is just a made up example). Whenever Victoria catches you watching Spanish bands on your laptop, she always comments and badmouths them in a sugar-coated way; she says things like "Umm… I don't mean this in an offensive way but I think Spanish guys are kind of girlish, they don't know how to dance and their songs are a little boring; that aside, they kind of all look the same unlike Italian guys who are hot dance kings". Even if Victoria added "I don't mean this in an offensive way", you are still hurt by her comment and you close your laptop and do something else.

The lesson for this chapter is that you should avoid the bad habit of criticizing other people's interests like Victoria does (especially when it's different than yours). Some people might like country music and they invest part of their lives appreciating it because they really do love it; if you go and bash country music and say things like "a bit boring; unlike rap music, which is fast and catchy", you will end up having that person hurt and annoyed. People will also hate your interests when you compare theirs to yours in such a way.

To recap this chapter,

Don't compare interests saying yours is better while pointing the flaws of the other's.

20. "Do you and your girlfriend..."

This is another thing that some people find annoying and some people don't, it's when your friends stick their heads in your private life and ask weird questions about you and your partner.

We're going to pretend that you're hanging out with a guy that you haven't seen in years. You currently have a beautiful girlfriend and he is still his own single self after all this time. You two talk while he browses your Facebook pictures and sees that you've got a nice girlfriend, he then bombards you with questions and asks things like "So do you and your girlfriend always..." while looking at you in a curious way. You want to punch his head in a friendly way but you manage to stay calm and stop him from asking anything more.

When you're with your friend, don't ask silly personal questions about their private lives. Sure, there are some girls that love it when people ask because they want to show off, but don't ask when you know it's a question that will irritate them.

To recap this chapter,

Don't ask curious private questions about your friend's boyfriend/girlfriend.

21.   Friends first... or was it smartphones first?

Being a good listener is something that raises your quality as a human being. You might think that people can only be annoyed at the things you say and the actions you do, but the way you listen to people can also make an impact on how they see you and how comfortable they are around you.

Story time! Jenny is spending the afternoon with this girl called Kate; Kate is very sad during that moment because she is having problems at work that are really making her stressed out. Kate talks to Jenny about her workplace and her workmates and every other thing that causes the problems in her life, she sighs and sniffles and wants Jenny to cheer her up, but what is Jenny doing? Jenny spends her time giggling and staring at her phone because she's absorbed in something else, Jenny then looks at Kate and realizes that Kate is silent and expecting something, so Jenny says "Well... aw... those bad things in life sure does suck", then she goes back to slowly giggling and using her phone, watching funny videos on her Facebook newsfeed. Kate then stands up and leaves and Jenny is confused not knowing what's wrong.

You don't want to be like Jenny. Jenny wasn't forced to listen, but at a time like that, she should have listened to her friend Kate and gave her some warm words to cheer her up.

This chapter's lesson is that you should always pay attention to your friends whenever they come to you to talk about their problems, if you're absorbed in something else while they're telling you their personal life, they're going to feel like you don't respect their life at all. I know I made a chapter earlier about people who always talk about their problems to everyone, but that's theirs to fix. Here are some tips you can use to become a better listener:

-Pay attention to what they're saying, show them that you care.
-Don't check your phone or laptop in the middle of the conversation; this makes them feel like their problems are worthless.
-Don't look around as if you were paying more attention to anything else other than them.
-Pick their side and cheer them up.
-Don't give flat uninterested answers such as "okay", "oh, too bad" etc.
-Don't make jokes when the person is serious.

To recap this chapter,

Listen carefully, pay attention and show that you care when your friend has a problem.

22. Whose toenail is this?

Don't you find it annoying when you come to your room and find some toenails on the floor? Bonus points if it's not yours.

We've all had those moments; this is one of those pet-peeves that get us both angry and grossed out.

Another example, let's say that you're going to take a shower. You prepare everything you need and get undressed, you whistle happily as you bring your shampoo and other accessories with you. Suddenly, you look down and see a dirty pair of panties in the shower room. The broomstick is now your best friend since you're going to use it to pick the panties up and put them away. Even after doing that, you still lost your desire to take a shower and decide to shower later.

It can also happen that you're so eager to go to the toilet and you have a bad habit of almost letting your needs out as you walk to the toilet because it feels good when your body tingles, but when you get to the toilet, the toilet is covered in piss (someone previously went wild and didn't clean up) you now lose your desire to use the toilet unless you wrap it up with thick toilet paper; in your case, there's no more.

The moral is to always clean up whenever you're done doing something considered dirty or "personal". People won't always be happy about finding your dirty things left around a shared place, be it a toilet, a shower room or something else.

To recap this chapter,

Clean up after you do something dirty (Remember, not everyone is your slave!)

23. Your friend loves you, but only for three hours

Unexpected company! Some people love it, some people don't. It can be great to have a friend come over and visit you if you're home alone on a boring day; if you already planned to do some things however, that friend can ruin your plans and you will have to choose another day to do whatever you had to do.

You don't want to be that friend who always comes unexpectedly and stays for a whole day at a friend's house. Sure, you two are probably best friends and all, but that friend probably has his/her own plans and it is very possible that you are the reason they could not do anything they planned to do that day.

When you plan to visit friends, make sure to give them a phone call beforehand and don't stay for too long since they might still have some things to do.

To recap this chapter,

Don't go to a friend's house without telling him/her first and don't stay for too long, they probably had plans for the day.

24. "Did I die?"

I know that a lot of you are not in the age of going to wild parties anymore, but I still included this in here for reference in case a younger audience is reading this book.

You and your friends all come to a party that a certain popular classmate invited you to. You have a friend Craig that can never manage to drink more than a glass of beer without getting drunk. Despite the fact that there will be alcohol, Craig still insists that he wants to go. In the end, you all accept to bring him over; when the time comes, Craig is drunk and makes the party crash by doing things that are crossing the line; he is the one who ended the party by standing on a table, throwing up around everyone and passing out. When the organizer asks who brought him over, people will point at you and you won't be able to go to anyone's party anymore because you brought someone like Craig.

Now the lesson is to not be like Craig, limit your alcohol consumption and pay attention to your behaviors, you might end up making your friends look bad if people knew that you're their friend.

To recap this chapter,

Don't get too wild and drunk at parties (I know some of you will disagree with this!).

25. "I'm fat, so is this hamburger"

We all have one friend like this; this behavior happens mostly with girls, but guys can have this problem too. It's the bad habit of constantly complaining about their weight (or any other problem) without putting a single effort into it (and sometimes even making it worse!).

It's Saturday and you don't have work; you decide to visit your friend Betty (How many names can you remember so far?). Betty and you are good friends and you spend the whole morning talking, chit chatting and doing activities together; there's one thing that bugs you about Betty however, she has been loading cakes in her plate and eating like a pig all morning; but that's not the issue, the issue is that every time she dips her spoon in the cake (she actually uses her hands to grab it), she complains to you about how fat she is and how unfair life is, she tells you things like "I wish I was skinny too" and "if only you could be in my shoes you would've been like this too" while devouring the cake like there's no tomorrow. You stare at her while nodding in a forced way (you're screaming internally), you want to help her but she will refuse to listen to any advice you give her.

Sometimes in life we do things that ruin us in a physical or emotional way; we tend to blame life or God or any other thing because of what we did to ourselves.

When you have a problem, locate its source and make sure that it's not because of you and your bad habits. If you're unusually gaining a lot of weight, review your diet (you might be addicted to chocolate cakes for example); if you're running low on money, review your expenses (you maybe have a bad habit of spending money on useless things).

The lesson for this chapter is to not complain too much around your friends when it is obvious that the problem is coming from you.

To recap this chapter,

Don't complain when you're not making an effort.

26. "Hey look, John's zippers are open!"

Have you ever been shamed publicly for something that you didn't actually do on purpose? Well... if yes, then you should already know that you shouldn't do the same to other people.

You're attending a formal after-work party with your friend Jennifer; Jennifer is the new employee and she has a hard time fitting-in with everyone else because she's new. An hour into the party, you notice that Jennifer forgot to remove the price tag on her dress; you know that it must be a new dress and that she must've been in a hurry because she almost got late for the party. You consider this a funny situation, and the way you handle the situation depends on how mature you currently are. So what do you do?

A: You say "Hey everyone!" catching their attention while giggling, you add "Jennifer is for sale for $45!" while pointing at her dress's price tag, wanting everyone to know that she forgot to take it off. Everyone bursts out laughing and you feel like a comedian; however, Jennifer feels upset after that and pretends to carry on for the night then leaves early, she then rarely talks to you at work after that.

The way you should handle it is:

B: You come to discreetly confront Jennifer about it and help her remove it; you probably didn't start a joke that got you praised for the night, but you saved a friend from dying of embarrassment.

So as the example showed you, it's better to save people from embarrassment than give them more of it.

To recap this chapter,

Don't publicly shame your friend if something is wrong with him/her or if they're doing something incorrectly.

27. Stop means Stop in English

This is something that a lot of people do that makes others mad or even fed up about them. It's when they're being told to stop doing something and still continue to do so.

We're going to take the example of a child first, since this behavior is more common in children. You have a kid and she likes to grab all the clothes from the drawer and throw it all on the ground; you ground her and tell her to stop it, but she keeps on doing it over and over no matter how many times you tell her to stop. It usually ends with a smack or something else.

Now let's take the adult example, you have a co-worker that constantly "messes with you in a fun way" by unplugging your keyboard every time you're going to the toilet. It's funny at first, but when he always does it, it becomes irritating and you can't focus on your work, it can even end up giving you stress at work. When you tell your co-worker about it, he just giggles and goes back to work because he thinks you're also having fun and that it's not that annoying, he doesn't think that you're fed up with it and he assumes that you're just having those "best friend" moments; but you're actually screaming internally.

The lesson for this chapter is that you should reconsider your habit of bugging your friends if they tell you to stop. If they do tell you something like "stop", they really mean it; they're not saying it while being playful with you.

To recap this chapter,

When someone asks you to stop something, they really mean it; stop and behave.

28. Not everybody should wake up at 4am

This is a very straightforward chapter, and you probably already know what it talks about.

This is something that once (or twice) happened to me and my family back in the good old days; I was still a young teenager and I used to stay up late. One day, my uncle visited and stayed for the night, I had my golden plans to stay in bed and wake up no earlier than 10am; however, as soon as the clock reached 4 a.m., my uncle's crazy alarm started to ring and I could hear it all the way to my room. It was one of the most frustrating ways to wake up after staying up so late, and I made sure that I will never do that to anyone else in the future.

When you set your alarm, don't set the ringtone volume too loud or you will risk of giving everyone in the house a bad morning.

To recap this chapter,

Don't use loud alarms that might wake everyone else in every other room.

29.   Cell phones don't need oil massage

This chapter is about using other people's belongings with dirty hands, or people using your belongings with their dirty hands.

Joe walks in your living room with a bag of chips and sits right next to you so he can watch whatever is going on TV together with you. Every now and then, Joe dips his fingers in his bag of chips and brings them to his lips, sometimes chewing and sucking on his cheesy fingers, sometimes not. Joe then suddenly remembers that he needed to check something on Amazon. He then asks you to lend him your phone just for a moment; you say "well sure, why not?" because you think it's something important and your friend needs help; but what happens next? Joe smiles widely with chips falling from his lips as he grabs your phone with hands full of oil and crust from the chips; the screen is now full of oil and your face is full of regret. Can you guess what he ordered on amazon? Twelve more bags of chips.

The lesson here is to wash your hands and make sure they're clean before you borrow and use someone else's phone, tablet or keyboard.

To recap this chapter,

Never use someone's phone/computer while your hands are dirty or greasy from eating food.

30. Movies are not meant to be interrupted

Yet another thing that always happens to me. It's always at that time that you're so concentrated on something that someone else comes in and bothers you with a lot of questions and stories.

You finally have the free time you need and decide to watch a movie that you've had for so long; you never had the time to watch it so now feels like the perfect moment to do so, you stream the movie on your TV/Laptop and you sit back and relax. Five minutes into the movie, your younger sister walks in and asks you if you know where her blue jacket is, you tell her to check in the living room and she walks away. Ten minutes later, she comes back in and asks you if she looks fat in her dress; of course you say no and move on to your movie, after five minutes, she comes back again and asks you some other favor and you lose all the concentration you had with the movie.

Now this does not have to be about movies, it could be that you were concentrating on your work, a personal finance report or something else; you just know that being constantly interrupted is tiring.

The lesson is to not interrupt anyone if you see and know that they are being concentrated on something, even if it is something recreational like a movie. Sometimes the thing you are going to bother them with is something that you can save for later or figure out by yourself.

To recap this chapter,

If someone is concentrated on something, do not constantly interrupt them.

31. Computer screens don't giggle

Non-techy friends, cousins, siblings etc., you name them. It might not be their fault since they don't know about it, but pointing and pressing on a computer screen with your finger is an irritating and dangerous move if you know why, and I am exactly going to tell you why.

Your computer screen is very different from a smartphone screen. A smartphone screen uses advanced glass technology (smartphones often use something called gorilla glass); it is a glass that is made to be used with your fingers and it can resist being scratched with metallic objects and being wet with a few water droplets; your computer screen however is very different, it is not protected with the same hard glass (even if it looks reflective) and pointing at it with your finger can cause clouds to form. What is a cloud? A cloud is a permanent white glow that appears on areas that have been affected by pressure and moisture. Since that cloud is permanent, your only chance is to replace the screen if that happens to you (some computer techs had some luck using sophisticated tools), so you better think twice before pointing at an LCD computer screen.

The lesson: don't press on a computer screen with your fingers, if you want to point something out then do it without touching the screen so it stays safe. If you know someone who has this bad habit, let them know about it.

To recap this chapter,

Never touch the screen on a computer.

32. "Tonight, we're eating cell phones."

You're probably familiar with the traditional manners that were applied back in the old days, but there are also new manners that you need to be aware of as time and technology progresses forward.

It's a beautiful Saturday night; it is Valentine's Day and your partner invited you (or you invited your partner) out for dinner. You imagined that it would be a long romantic night where you will spend most of the time talking about your life together and deepening your connection with your partner by talking and giggling the whole time; but guess what actually happens? Your partner spends most of the time on the cell phone and checks the internet for new notifications on Facebook and twitter; right after you two are done eating, your partner stands up and that's it for the night.

When you are on a date night with someone or if you are taking someone out for dinner, avoid using your cellphone too much (or at all!) since it will create a gap between you two because you are too sucked in your cell phone as if your partner did not exist or as if the people in your cell phone were more important than your partner.

This does not apply only for romantic dinners but for family dinners and other occasions where you need to give people your attention as well.

To recap this chapter,

Don't use your phone while dining with someone.

33. Showing off your friend's belongings to your friends

Your friend looks so mighty, he walks into a room and all of your friends look at him amazed that he has a real Rolando jacket (before you do a Google search, Rolando is just a made up brand). He says things like "oh, this only cost me $500, not a big deal" and pretends to be super chill about it. The real issue here is not that he has a $500 jacket; it's that it's not even his, it's yours, and he didn't tell you that he would be showing it off to everyone when he borrowed it.

Sometimes we secretly do this to our friends' belongings whenever something looks good on us. This is a bad thing because you're taking credit for someone else's belongings, just like that time you stole a friend's joke and repeated it in a higher voice. It can be annoying to watch someone take your stuff and pretend it's theirs and get praised somewhere. When it's your time to wear or bring whatever great thing you own, people are going to say "oh you borrowed that from him right?" when in fact, you're the actual owner.

This is pretty straightforward, but when you borrow something from a friend, don't show off pretending that it's yours.

To recap this chapter,

Don't take credit for something you borrowed from a friend.

34. Mr. CEO's secretary

You hate them, I do too. It's the people who try to make you look bad in front of your boss so that the boss loves them more than you. It's not like you have a thing for your boss, it's just that that person is being unfair and straightly annoying.

Say you're late at work and your boss scolds you, you try to desperately tell the boss that it was not your fault, but your annoying co-worker Brianna gives you a harder time by saying things like "oh, this is something usual", "always late for work", "must've woken up late again, not caring about work" and many other irritating things. Whenever you do something wrong and the boss is there, she points out all of your flaws and compares you to herself by saying "unlike me, who's always on time, organized etc." Her goal is probably not to degrade you, but to make herself look better. By doing this however, she essentially makes you look bad.

Work hard and let your actions define how great you are in your office instead of degrading your co-workers just to make yourself look like the example employee.

To recap this chapter,

Don't be an annoying co-worker by trying to make yourself your boss' favorite employee.

35. A thumbs up isn't worth a thousand words

If you use Facebook or any other social networking sites with this feature, you probably already know what I am talking about.

You haven't talked to your friend for almost one whole year and you wanted to get a lively conversation going, you send a message that says "Hey Stacy! How's it going? We haven't been talking for almost a year, is everything okay there? Are you alright over there? John and I moved to this new apartment in Madison and so far everything is fine here, I hope to hear back from you. Looking at your pictures, I can see that you have really changed in such a short time! Well that's all for now, talk to you later!" You were huffing and puffing as you wrote the long text, you even proofread your text so that everything looks neat and nice, but what happens after you send it? Stacy replies with just one big "thumbs-up" indicating that she got your message and that she has read it. She didn't add anything else at all and you feel like you've just wasted your time and effort into that message just to get a "thumbs-up".

The lesson for you is to never reply to long messages with just a single word like "k" or "okay" or "mm", or anything like a thumbs-up (which is a common thing with today's social networks). This makes the person feel like you totally don't care about them or whatever they said. You should only use those when you two are closing a discussion.

To recap this chapter,

Never reply a long message by a simple "thumbs up" or a "Kay".

36. "You think you had a bad day? Last time I..."

When something bad happens to us, we are eager to tell everyone about our story. We expect people to show us sympathy, but sometimes, the exact opposite happens.

Imagine that you had a hard day; your car refused to start in the morning and you had to take the bus, on your way to the bus, a motorcycle crashed into you and now you're in the hospital. After some while, your friends and family come to visit you, they are sorry to hear that you got in an accident and feel bad for you, but there's always that one person that wants to be

Mr. Interesting and says things like "Well, it's pretty sad, but last time I had a day that was even worse! It all started when..." that person then proceeds to share his unfortunate story and tries to get everyone to feel sorry for him too (as if it was cool in any way).

When somebody is having a bad time, we are tempted to share our past experiences as well, attempting to make them feel better as if their misfortune was nothing, but when we do this, we don't know that the person feels hurt, they don't want to hear about you. When you share your experience, you're indirectly defying their case and you're essentially saying "well what are you so sad about? It's not that much of a big deal and mine should be heard out because mine is more interesting".

You don't want to steal the attention away from somebody else especially at times like this, if you have a friend that was injured or troubled, just support them and show them that you care.

To recap this chapter,

Support your friend and don't say you've gone through worse, making it all about you.

37. "I used to be good at drawing too"

I know, I know, you hate the fact that everyone finds your friend awesome because she is very good at drawing. That does not mean that you will get the same praise if you tell everyone that you too, used to be good at drawing.

John and Steven are on the table with their friends; Steven's phone rings and he starts to speak French with his family on the phone and everyone looks at him amazed since they don't have a single idea what he is talking about. When the call ends, John wants to be Mr. Interesting and tells Steven "oh you speak French too? I used to speak French before and I also learned Spanish and Italian back in school". Nobody really asked John if he knew how to speak French or Spanish or whatever but John still said it because he saw that everyone was amazed at Steven and he wanted to get some of that attention too.

When you're with some friends and one friend shows some nice unique skill, let him get his praise; it might as well be the only quality he has so you should not steal his moment. People admire the qualities that you currently have, not the qualities you "used to" have. You can tell everyone that you used to be good at this and that but they will like it better if they saw you demonstrating your skills to prove that you're not just all talk.

To recap this chapter,

When a friend has a unique skill, don't try to steal the show by telling everyone that you used to be good at it too.

38. Adult manners should be child manners

You may have grown up, but you should always remember that adult manners should be the same as good child manners.

It is very possible that you've forgotten a lot of the manners that have been taught to you when you were a child because you think that as you grow up, you don't need them anymore to be respected, but you're totally wrong! When I say adult manners should be child manners, I want you to know that you should always have good manners just like you did when you were a child.

When you cough, cover your mouth; when you sneeze, cover your face; when you eat, don't chew with your mouth open; when you talk to people, don't be rude and assume they will respect your rude behaviors because you're older. Always remember and respect the manners that were taught to you when you were a child, they were not just temporary.

To recap this chapter,

You should still have good manners even when you're already an adult.

39. "Our toilet, my rules"

This is a common thing that happens in shared places (work offices, family homes etc.). There is always one person who seems to never respect the rules in the house when it comes to things that are shared between others (co-workers, siblings etc.), and always gets everyone pissed because of it.

Let's jump straight to the example; everyone in the house is taught a set of rules: guys have to pull the toilet seat up before pissing and put it back down when they're done; girls however don't need to pull anything but they will have to clean up after they do their "girly" things. A perfect example of a rule breaker would be a guy that pisses all over the toilet seat without pulling it up first; it annoys the girls in the house and they are forced to clean his mess in order to sit on the toilet without getting wet. Another example would be a girl that leaves all of her bloody matter on the floor after "changing" some of her "stuff"; as natural as it is, it will be an eyesore for the others if they saw it left on the floor.

Would you like it if you had an urge to use the toilet but it is full of someone else's "lemon juice" so you can't sit down? If not then do not to make other people suffer the same thing.

To recap this chapter,

Know that others use the toilet, bathroom etc. too. Don't be too nasty.

40. "I'll buy you another one / I'll replace it later"

Do you know someone like this? Someone who is rich or perhaps someone who struggles to make money yet says things like this? Sometimes, people tend to not care about others' belongings and assume that they can replace everything with money if ever they "accidentally" broke it or took it.

Your annoying rich friend comes over to visit you; he sees some sweets on the table and opens them without even asking you. When he sees you entering the room, he tells you "oh I ate your biscuits but I'll buy you another one" while eating them; little did he know that those were biscuits you affectionately bought for your nephews. After some chit chatting, it's time for him to go home; on his way to the door, he suddenly remembers something and tells you "oh yeah, sorry I accidentally broke the screen of the laptop I borrowed from you, I'll give you some money later so it's okay". You ask yourself "you will replace it, but when?" You know that it's not about the money, not about replacing things, you probably need the laptop before the time he replaces it, and it's possible that you had some personal attachment to whatever thing he just ate/broke and money can't replace it. Whatever your reason is, it's normal that you feel irritated and annoyed by this behavior.

After this chapter, I want you to think of your habits. Can you relate to the rich guy in the story? If yes then you should avoid that habit of thinking that you can replace anything because you have the money and power to do so. Some things might have personal value that money can't replace. You're not going to eat and replace someone else's valentine's chocolate because there was love put into it and it's not the same thing anymore even if you buy some new chocolates.

To recap this chapter,

Never say "I'll buy you another one" and take someone's belongings/food, money can't replace everything.

41. "They don't use it right away, therefore, they don't care about it"

Uncles and older people usually do this, but young kids too tend to assume that things that are sitting around for some time are being abandoned by their owners.

This happened to me; I had a bicycle that I didn't use for a whole month. During that time, some construction workers were working on a house that was right next to mine. In the country I was in, you leave your car and bicycles on the front yard (of course, you need to lock them), so the construction workers kept seeing my beautiful road racing bicycle just sitting around all the time. What they didn't know is that the bicycle was only unused for one month and they were only working on the house during that month so they thought it was just sitting there since a long time. One day, I went to an important meeting that was held in the city center (so I took a long time away), when I came back, the bike was gone, and even the heavy frame that was used to lock it was cut with some metal cutting tools. I was so disappointed since it was a gift from my eldest brother and I really loved it.

This can happen with food too, if you put a cake in the fridge with the intent to save it for when the night comes (when you'll be watching a movie), another person who constantly opens the fridge will see the cake every hour and that person might end up assuming that nobody is going to eat it anymore since nobody cares about it. When the night comes, you open the fridge and you see that your cake is gone. You are now disappointed and you start your investigation on who ate it.

So the lesson for this chapter is to always ask about things that you find lying around, the owner probably doesn't need it for the moment, but they will still use it sometime later. Don't go and take other people's things even if you think they're just wasting it, ask first.

To recap this chapter,

If you see something unused, chances are that the owner still needs it.

42. "It's free because he's my friend"

A big mistake that people usually do when they have a friend who is skilled in one field is to assume that that friend would do anything for them for free because it's a friend. This happened to me personally, and I don't want it to happen to anyone else, so I made sure not to forget to write a chapter about it.

One time, this old guy (who was sort of a friend of mine, but he was not that close) dropped his laptop at my place because it was filled with viruses and he didn't know what to do about it. At that time, I was known as the local IT guy and everyone would just drop their stuff at my home and give me a small commission in exchange for fixing their machines, but this guy, he would just walk off with a dry "thanks man, you guys are lucky you know this stuff" every time I finish fixing his computers and he would come back again next time, all without giving me a single penny. I was not frustrated because I wanted a lot of money, it's because I lost some of my time that I should've been putting to work, yet he gave nothing valuable in return and I felt like I was just being used for free. He failed to acknowledge that I needed to make a living too and that it's not just as simple as pushing buttons.

I want to say hi to all of the artists out there as well; I know you guys get a lot of "you're very good at drawing, can you draw me?" every time, yet people will shy away if you said it was not for free. They fail to acknowledge that you worked hard for your skills and that you need to make a living too (if art is your main job).

So the lesson for this chapter, don't ask your friends for free services if it is a trade they're skilled in and that it's something of quality that takes time and patience.

To recap this chapter,

If you ask a professional service, don't assume it will be free because the person is your friend.

43. Just answer their question, it's their decision

Sometimes, people tend to lecture you based on their personal opinions when you ask them a question about something that you might not even do. Without knowing it, they are doing something that can irritate the person they are talking to.

You for example, ask your friend if she knows any bungee jumping clubs around your place since you don't know any and it's possible that you were just being curious or that it is for a friend, not for yourself. She then looks at you with a weird face and tells you "bungee jumping? Why the hell would you look for such a dangerous activity? I also find it stupid that you're being hanged on a rope and thrown off a bridge; if I were you, I would be better doing bowling". You then regret ever asking her and you keep any questions to yourself from that time on.

When people ask you questions, they of course want to hear something that answers that question. If you drive them off and criticize whatever they are asking about, you are essentially criticizing their interests and they end up regretting ever asking you; you become unreliable that time.

Answer the question or tell them that you don't know if you don't know about the topic that they are asking about.

To recap this chapter,

Don't say "why would you want to know about…" when a friend asks something, answer them.

44. "No offence" means "I'm going to hurt you"

I am taking a guess that I am not the only one who notices this, but when people say "no offence", it makes things even worse.

I am not going to give a lot of details for this chapter since the title is already enough to explain what I mean, but whenever you want to make a remark, don't include the traditional "no offence" introduction before saying something offensive, adding those words will only make the person mentally prepare for an offensive insult or remark and it adds weight to the rudeness of your following words.

"No offence but I think your shoes are lame", "no offence but you look ugly", "no offence but I don't like your kids' teeth", you name your own examples, and you know that adding "no offence" only makes it worse .

To recap this chapter,

Saying "No offence but…" is going to make something sound more hurtful.

Printed in Great Britain
by Amazon